SCIENCE SURPRISES ™

EVERYDAY PHYSICAL SCIENCE EXPERIMENTS WITH
GASES

AMY FRENCH MERRILL

The Rosen Publishing Group's
PowerKids Press ™
New York

For Shane

Some of the experiments in this book are designed for a child to do with an adult.

Published in 2002 by The Rosen Publishing Group, Inc.
29 East 21st Street, New York, NY 10010

First Edition

Book Design: Michael Caroleo and Michael de Guzman
Layout: Nick Sciacca
Project Editor: Frances E. Ruffin

Photo Credits: p. 5 (boy) © Skjold Photography, (eagle) © Digital Stock, (landscape) © EyeWire; all experiment photos by Adriana Skura.

Merrill, Amy French.
Everyday physical science experiments with gases / Amy French Merrill—1st ed.
    p. cm. — (Science surprises)
Includes bibliographical references and index.
  ISBN 0-8239-5803-5 (lib. bdg.)
  1. Gases—Experiments—Juvenile literature. [1. Gases—Experiments. 2. Experiments.] I. Title. II. Series.
  QC161.2 .M47 2002
  530.4'3'078—dc21

                                                            00-013049

Manufactured in the United States of America

CONTENTS

IT'S A GAS

It's invisible. Birds fly through it. It surrounds us. People, plants, and animals use it every day. What is it? It's the air!

Stick out your tongue. Can you taste the air? No. Hold out your hands. Can you catch the air? No. You can't smell air or see air, either. Now spin around with your arms held wide. You can feel the air move against your skin.

Air is a gas. Many gases don't have a smell or a taste. Most gases are invisible, too. A gas is a form of **matter** that doesn't have a definite or permanent shape or **volume**.

So how do we know that gases are really there? Read on to find out!

Many living things need the gases that are in the air to breathe, to make food, or to grow. ▶

AIR IS EVERYWHERE

Is an empty glass really empty? Try this experiment. Stuff a paper towel tightly into the bottom of a glass. Make sure that it stays there even when you turn the glass upside down. Next fill a sink or a large bowl with water. Turn the glass upside down, hold it straight, and plunge it into the water. Count to five. Then lift the glass out of the water without tilting it. Pull the paper towel out of the glass. What happened?

MATERIALS NEEDED:
glass, paper towel, sink or bowl full of water

The paper in the glass stayed dry because the water could not rise up and get into the glass. Why? Because the glass was already full. It was full of air!

How do we know gases are really there? Like the air in the glass, all gases take up space. ▶

A gas will fill any size or shape of container. ▶

What Is a Gas?

Like all forms of matter, gases are made up of **molecules**. The air around us has molecules of different kinds of gases. Some of the molecules in air are **oxygen**, one of the most important gases. We couldn't live without oxygen. Without oxygen, we would not be able to produce **energy**. Oxygen is also present when things burn. Try this experiment. Pour colored water into a large glass bowl. Place a candle firmly into a candleholder. Place the candle and holder into the bowl. Have an adult light the candle for you. Cover the lit

MATERIALS NEEDED:
large bowl, water, glass jar, candle, candleholder, food coloring

◀ *The flame on a candle needs oxygen to burn.*

candle with a glass jar. What happens? The water inside the glass jar will rise a few inches. Then the flame on the candle will go out. Why? The flame uses up all the oxygen in the jar. The water level moves up to fill in the space, or volume, that the oxygen occupies before it burns off.

When the candle goes out, the water level rises to replace the used up oxygen. The only gas left in the jar is nitrogen. ▶

GIVE IT A SQUEEZE

Unlike solids or liquids, gas molecules are spaced widely apart and they move around freely at great speed. It is possible to squeeze molecules of gas together, though. Try this. Find an empty plastic bottle and screw on the cap tightly. Of course, the bottle isn't really empty. It's full of air. Like all gases, air can be **compressed.** Squeeze the bottle to compress the air that is in it. The molecules in a compressed gas are packed tightly and they move very closely together.

MATERIALS NEEDED:
plastic bottle with a cap, water, funnel, food coloring

10

Use a funnel to fill the same bottle with colored water. Make sure it is completely full of water before you put the cap back on. Squeeze the bottle. What happens? It can't be squeezed! The molecules in liquids cannot be compressed the way they can in gases.

The molecules in a gas are widely separated and move at great speed. Liquids and solids ▶ *have more tightly packed molecules .*

A Mass of Gas

Gases are one of the **states** of matter. Three states of matter are solid, liquid, and gas. Here's an experiment that involves all of them.

Use a funnel to put two large spoonfuls of baking soda into a balloon. Fill a small bottle halfway with vinegar. Without letting any of the baking soda fall into the bottle, carefully stretch the neck of the balloon over the bottle's opening. When the balloon is tightly stretched over the bottle, hold the balloon up so that the baking soda falls into the bottle.

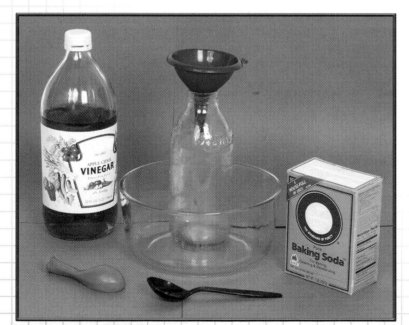

Mixing baking soda and vinegar produces a chemical reaction.

Wow! What happens?
A gas is formed.
Baking soda is a solid and vinegar is a liquid. When these two items mix, they produce a gas called **carbon dioxide**. There isn't enough room for the gas in the bottle, so its molecules rise up from the bottle and fill the balloon.

When the molecules of carbon dioxide gas expand, they become more widely spaced and move rapidly. The bottle can no longer contain them.

WATCH WATER FORM

Most gases change to a liquid state when they are cooled. This process is called **condensation**. When gases are cooled, their molecules slow down and stick together. By sticking together, they become a liquid. Have you ever breathed on a cold window? A gas called **water vapor** is created by your breath. It condenses into drops of water on the window.

Here's an experiment that shows how a gas becomes a liquid. Place several pieces of ice in a large glass jar and fill

MATERIALS NEEDED:

large glass jar, shaved ice or ice cubes, spoon

14

Clouds are produced when air contains a lot of water vapor. When the water vapor in clouds condenses, this produces droplets of rain.

the glass jar with water. Leave the jar alone for several minutes and then check on it. Drops of water appear on the outside of the glass jar! This happens because the ice is cold. The air around the jar becomes cool, too. As the air cools, it condenses and forms drops of water on the glass jar.

Does the water on the outside of the glass jar feel cold to the touch? ▶

A Cycle of Gases

There are many different gases. The air that we breathe is a mixture of gases. Two important gases in the air are oxygen and carbon dioxide. People take in oxygen when they breathe in, and they give off carbon dioxide when they breathe out.

In a process called **photosynthesis**, green plants use energy from sunlight and produce food from carbon dioxide and water. You can see part of this process. Place some freshly cut leaves in a clear container full of water. Make sure the water covers the leaves entirely. Then leave the container in a place

MATERIALS NEEDED:

container of water,
freshly cut plant leaves

When humans and animals breathe out, they give off carbon dioxide, which is used by plants for food.

where it will get sunlight for a few days. What happens? You can see bubbles of oxygen appear on the leaves of the plant. This is because plants take in carbon dioxide and give off oxygen. Then people breathe in the oxygen. This exchange of gases is called the carbon dioxide and oxygen cycle.

The bubbles that you see on the plants are bubbles of oxygen. People need oxygen to live.

What Is that Fizz?

A **solution** is formed when the molecules of a gas, liquid, or solid are mixed and spread evenly throughout another liquid or gas (or even a solid). A soft drink is a solution of a liquid and carbon dioxide gas. A special machine at a soft drink factory pumps the carbon dioxide into the drink. Then the drink is sealed in a can or bottle. The hiss you hear when you open a soft drink is the sound of gas escaping!

MATERIALS NEEDED:

pitcher, 2 cups (473 ml) water, 2 tablespoons (30 ml) powdered sugar, 3 tablespoons (44 ml) baking soda, 6 teaspoons (30 ml) lemon juice, food coloring (optional)

In this solution, the carbon dioxide gas dissolves into the water.

You can make your own soft drink. Here's how. Add 2 cups (473 ml) of water to a pitcher. Add 2 tablespoons (30 ml) of powdered sugar, and, if you'd like, add a few drops of food coloring. Stir in 3 tablespoons (44 ml) of baking soda. Then add 6 teaspoons (30 ml) of lemon juice. Stir the mixture. It should start to bubble. You've created soda pop.

Pour your soda pop into a glass and enjoy it! ▶

AIR PRESSURE

Did you realize that you live at the bottom of an ocean? Well, you do. You live at the bottom of an ocean of air. It's called the **atmosphere**. The atmosphere is made up of all the gases that surround Earth.

Earth's atmosphere is over 50 miles (80 km) thick. That's a lot of air! All that air creates **pressure**. Air pressure is not always the same. Scientists measure changes in air pressure with a tool called a **barometer**. Barometers are used to tell changes in the weather. High air pressure usually means good weather. Low air pressure often can bring high winds and storms.

MATERIALS NEEDED:
round balloon, scissors, small jar or bottle, rubber band, drinking straw, tape, index card, pen

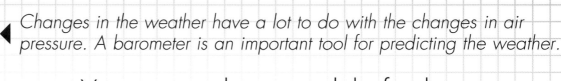

You can make a model of a barometer. Cut the neck off a round balloon and stretch it over a small jar or bottle. Fasten the balloon tightly around the jar with a rubber band. Cut a drinking straw in half. Tape one end of the straw to the center of the balloon. Tape an index card to a wall and set your barometer near the card. Mark the height of the straw on the card at the same time every day for a week. The straw moves up when air pressure increases. Look for good weather. The straw moves down as air pressure decreases. There might be a storm ahead.

After a week of observing the changes on your barometer, were you able to give some prediction about the weather? ▶

WHAT A GAS!

There are many different kinds of gases, and they are used in all sorts of ways. Air is a mixture of gases that are necessary to living things. People also use gas for energy. It is a **fuel**. Some gases heat buildings and homes. They are used for cooking food on gas stoves and for powering large appliances such as clothes dryers.

Gases are used just for fun, too. Have you ever seen a hot air balloon? Gases are used in these balloons to carry people high in the sky! Helium gas makes birthday balloons rise and float in the air. We use the air to blow bubbles, throw paper airplanes, and fly kites. What a gas!

GLOSSARY

atmosphere (AT-muh-sfeer) The layer of gases that surrounds an object in space. On Earth, this layer is air.

barometer (buh-RAH-meh-tur) A tool used to measure changes in air pressure.

carbon dioxide (KAR-bin dy-OK-syd) A gas that plants take in from the air and use to make food.

compressed (kum-PRESD) To have squeezed something into a smaller space.

condensation (kon-den-SAY-shun) Cooled gas that has turned into droplets of liquid.

energy (EH-nur-jee) The ability to do work.

fuel (FYOOL) Something used to make energy, warmth, or power.

matter (MA-ter) The material that makes up something

molecules (MAH-li-kyoolz) Tiny building blocks that make up a substance.

oxygen (AHK-sih-jin) A gas in the air that has no color, taste, or odor, and is necessary for people and animals to breathe.

photosynthesis (foh-toh-SIN-thuh-sis) The process in which plants use energy from sunlight, gases from air, and water from soil to make food and release oxygen.

pressure (PREH-shur) A force that pushes on something.

solution (suh-LOO-shun) A mixture of two substances, one of which dissolves in the other.

states (STAYTS) Forms that matter can take—solid, liquid, or gas.

volume (VOL-yoom) How much space matter takes up.

water vapor (WAH-ter VAY-pur) The gas state of water.

INDEX

WEB SITES

To learn more about gases, check out this Web site:
http://library.thinkquest.org/2690/exper/exper.htm